IT'S MY STATE!

UTAH

Doug Sanders

Lisa M. Herrington

Marshall Cavendish
Benchmark
New York

Library of Congress Cataloging-in-Publication Data
     Sanders, Doug, 1972-
     Utah / Doug Sanders, Lisa M. Herrington. — 2nd ed.
        p. cm. — (It's my state!)
     Includes bibliographical references and index.
     Summary: "Surveys the history, geography, government, economy, and people of Utah"—Provided by publisher.
     ISBN 978-1-60870-659-4 (print) — ISBN 978-1-60870-814-7 (ebook)
     1. Utah—Juvenile literature. I. Herrington, Lisa M. II. Title.
  F826.3.S36 2013
  979.2—dc23   2011020741

Second Edition developed for Marshall Cavendish Benchmark by RJF Publishing LLC (www.RJFpublishing.com)
Series Designer, Second Edition: Tammy West/Westgraphix LLC
Editor, Second Edition: Amanda Hudson

All maps, illustrations, and graphics © Marshall Cavendish Corporation. Maps and artwork on pages 6, 26, 27, 75, 76, and back cover by Christopher Santoro. Map and graphics on pages 10 and 44 by Westgraphix LLC.

The photographs in this book are used by permission and through the courtesy of:
Front cover: Ron Brown/Superstock and Aurora Photos/Alamy (inset).
Alamy: Tom Mareschal, 4 (left); National Geographic Image Collection, 5; blickwinkel, 11; Marco Regalia Sell, 12; Goddard Automotive, 13; Jon Arnold Image Ltd., 14 (top); offiwent.com, 14 (bottom); Rolf Richardson, 15; Laura Romin & Larry Dalton, 21 (left); Scott Warren, 22; Prisma Bildagentur AG, 24; Chris Howes/Wild Places Photography, 25; North Wind Picture Archives, 29, 31, 34; World History Archive, 35; Everett Collection Inc, 37; Tetra Images, 42; The Art Archive, 48 (left); Utah Images, 50; Rob Crandall, 52, 62; Douglas Pulsipher, 54, 69; Megapress, 65; amana images inc., 66; science photos, 67; Sunpix Travel, 70 (bottom); Whit Richardson, 73; H. Mark Weidman Photography, 74. **Associated Press:** Associated Press, 40, 46, 47, 48 (right), 49, 53, 57, 58. **Getty Images:** AFP, 39; Lori Adamski Peek, 45; Bloomberg, 51 (top); Getty Images, 51 (bottom); Barry Wong, 64. **Superstock:** Science Faction, 4 (right), 17; Mauritius, 8; Painted Sky Images, 16; age fotostock, 18; Tier und Naturfotografie, 19; George Ostertag, 20; Minden Pictures, 21 (right), 71; Hoberman Collection, 32; Stock Connection, 60; imagebroker.net, 70 (top). **Utah State Historical Society:** Used by permission, Utah State Historical Society, all rights reserved, 28.

Printed in Malaysia (T).
135642

CONTENTS

A Quick Look at UTAH

State Tree: Blue Spruce

A popular choice for Christmas trees, the blue spruce was adopted as the state tree on February 20, 1933. The bill was passed by the legislature in record time because concerned citizens wanted to be sure they beat neighbor Colorado in adopting this state symbol.

State Bird: California Seagull

The California seagull is an important part of the state's lore. The bird is said to have saved Mormon pioneers' crops in 1848 by eating swarms of hungry crickets invading the fields. The event has come to be known as the Miracle of the Gulls. A world-class insect gobbler, the seagull breeds and often winters on inland lakes, including the state's massive Great Salt Lake. In honor of this bird, a statue called the Seagull Monument was erected in Salt Lake City, the state capital.

State Flower: Sego Lily

In 1911, Utah's schoolchildren chose the sego lily as the state flower. The graceful flower grows in the open rangeland of the state's Basin and Range region. The bulbs were eaten by the state's American Indian population, as well as by Mormon settlers during their first grueling winter in the area.

State Animal: Rocky Mountain Elk

This hoofed mammal usually summers in the mountains and spends the winter grazing Utah's valleys. A member of the deer family, the Rocky Mountain elk was made the official state animal on February 1, 1971.

State Fossil: *Allosaurus*

Many *Allosaurus* fossils have been found in Utah. An average *Allosaurus* weighed 2 tons (1.8 metric tons) and was about 30 feet (9 meters) long. These fearsome dinosaurs were among the most successful meat-eaters of the late Jurassic period.

State Insect: Honey Bee

Before it became nicknamed the Beehive State, Utah was once known as the Provisional State of Deseret. *Deseret* is a Mormon word that means "honey bee." This hardworking insect symbolized the perseverance of the early Mormon settlers. The honey bee officially became the state insect in 1983.

The Beehive State

For those who love the outdoors, Utah is a paradise. This western state is home to five national parks, seven national monuments, two national recreation areas, and six national forests. With a land area of 82,144 square miles (212,752 square kilometers), Utah ranks twelfth in size among the states. Although large, it would still take three Utahs to fit inside Texas. Utah is divided into twenty-nine counties.

In 1849, Utah's first white settlers—the Mormons—called their new state Deseret, a Mormon word for "honey bee." Bees represented the hard work of those early pioneers. Utah was later nicknamed the Beehive State. A beehive appears on the state flag and seal. It is also on the official state emblem.

Utah offers a full range of breathtaking natural wonders to explore. Wind and water have carved amazing rock formations over millions of years. Looping arches and natural bridges are among the state's incredible sights.

Rock cliffs tower high above the flat deserts, which seem to be empty. But in the summer months, animals tend to be more active at sunset, finally free of the day's heat. As the sun dips into the west, the rock walls seem to glow in the red-orange light.

Quick Facts

UTAH BORDERS

North	Idaho
	Wyoming
South	Arizona
East	Colorado
	Wyoming
West	Nevada

The scenic Uinta Mountains are a popular place to hike, fish, and hunt. Most of the mountains lie within the Ashley National Forest.

Snow-capped peaks of the Rocky Mountains jut straight into the sky. Utah inspires a sense of awe in visitors and residents alike. It is not surprising why. With its three main regions, Utah is truly a land of contrasts and dazzling beauty.

Rocky Mountains

The Rocky Mountains spread over a large part of western North America, extending from Canada in the north to Mexico in the south. The Uinta and Wasatch mountain ranges make up part of the Rocky Mountains in Utah.

The Uintas stretch across the northeastern corner of the state, running west from Colorado for about 150 miles (240 kilometers). They reach almost as far as Salt Lake City in north-central Utah. Named after the Ute Indians, the Uintas are a unique group of mountains. The Uintas are the only mountain range in North America that spread in an east-west direction. The spines of all the continent's other mountain chains line up north to south. But what makes the Uintas truly original is their striking beauty. Their rounded, snow-capped peaks are hard to miss in this part of the state.

The Wasatch Mountains start around Mount Nebo, near the center of the state, and extend north for about 250 miles (400 km) into parts of southeastern Idaho. They are a popular spot for skiers, snowboarders, and mountain bikers. The eastern edge of the Wasatch starts as valleys and rolling plains. These slowly give way to high peaks and jagged irregular plateaus, or areas of raised land. During the last Ice Age, which ended about 11,000 years ago, massive sheets of slow-moving ice

Quick Facts

HIGHEST AND LOWEST
The highest point in Utah is Kings Peak. Located in the heart of the Uinta Mountains, in Duchesne County, it stands 13,528 feet (4,123 m) tall. The Beaver Dam Wash area, in Washington County in the southwestern corner of Utah, has the state's lowest point, at about 2,180 feet (664 m) above sea level. Beaver Dam Wash is a stream that flows for part of the year but runs dry at other times.

Utah Counties

Utah has 29 counties.

called glaciers cut deep canyons in this rugged ever-changing range. But perhaps its most striking feature is the steep western edge. There the mountains loom from 6,000 to 8,000 feet (1,800 to 2,400 m) above the valleys below. This sheer mountain wall is known as the Wasatch Front. Below this, the Basin and Range region begins.

Basin and Range Region

The Basin and Range region is located in the western part of the state. This region makes up Utah's desert country. Spreading for miles, the sandy stretches of the Sevier and Escalante deserts located here are among the driest places in the United States. These broad valleys, also known as basins, separate several impressive mountains that run north to south. Smaller mountain ranges mixed in with wide rounded basins are grouped in the center of the region. To the east and west of the Basin and Range region, the elevation starts to climb. Dusty plateaus give rise to larger mountain chains. They offer some of Utah's best soaring views.

In the northeastern part of the region lies the Great Salt Lake. This large body of water is about 75 miles (120 km) long and 35 miles (55 km) wide. The

Quick Facts

TINY INHABITANTS
No fish species are able to survive in the Great Salt Lake. Tiny brine shrimp are the only creatures that can live in the salty water. They are harvested and processed into fish food.

The Great Salt Lake is the saltiest lake in North America. Few living creatures can survive in it.

Great Salt Lake covers more than a million acres (405,000 hectares), or about 2,100 square miles (5,440 sq km). It is the largest natural lake west of the Mississippi River, and it is the largest saltwater lake in North America. It gets its name because the lake is saltier than the oceans. Dissolved minerals empty into the Great Salt Lake through four rivers and several streams. With no rivers or streams flowing out of the Great Salt Lake, large deposits of salt build up in the water. Companies now take salt from the lake and use it for a variety of purposes. The salt used on icy roadways, for instance, may come from the Great Salt Lake.

The Great Salt Lake is a remnant of a giant, ancient lake called Lake Bonneville. For thousands of years the water level rose and fell, until finally the lake dried up almost completely. What remained was a group of smaller lakes and a desert covered with salt and hard-caked soil. The Great Salt Lake Desert

START YOUR ENGINES!

With its rock-hard surface, the Bonneville Salt Flats, in northwestern Utah, is an ideal spot for race-car drivers to attempt to break world speed records. Since 1914, hundreds of records have been set and broken on this stretch of flat, hard land.

is famous for its salt beds. Today, the Bonneville Salt Flats cover parts of this desert. This vast stretch of smooth, white land is named after Lake Bonneville. It covers about 30,000 acres (12,140 ha).

Colorado Plateau

Utah's third natural region is the Colorado Plateau. This vast and varied region extends from the Uinta Basin to the high plateaus and deep canyons that mark southern Utah. The Uinta Basin is a bowl-shaped area located south of the Uinta Mountains. The Colorado Plateau covers more than half of the state—most of eastern and southern Utah. But the entire plateau stretches far beyond Utah's borders. It includes parts of Colorado, Arizona, and New Mexico.

The Colorado Plateau has a mix of features. High plateaus and mountains more than 11,000 feet (3,350 m) tall mark the western part of the region. These upland plains, as they are sometimes called, are not the flat and smooth places people usually think of as plains. Striped cliffs with pink, white, and red layers jut out of the land. Parts of the plateau are marked by curves folding into wondrous shapes. Ridges and mesas—flat-topped hills or mountains with steep sides—are

Bryce Canyon National Park covers more than 37,000 acres (15,000 ha) in the southwestern part of the state.

bordered here and there by canyons, gorges, and valleys. Zion, Bryce, and Cedar Breaks are some of the well-known canyons that add to the area's unique appearance. In the southeastern part of the state, the Colorado River is met by the Green River. These are the state's two main rivers. They have helped to carve out some of Utah's deepest canyons.

Rainbow Bridge is just one of the spectacular landforms located in the southern part of the state. It is the world's largest known bridge of natural rock, standing 278 feet (85 m) wide and

Rainbow Bridge is one of Utah's most popular tourist attractions.

309 feet (94 m) high. Rainbow Bridge was formed when water eroded the sandstone. Nestled among the canyons, it is considered a sacred place by the Navajo tribe. The natural stone arch is accessible from Lake Powell, the second largest human-made lake in the world. The lake was created when Glen Canyon Dam was constructed on the Colorado River in Arizona. Construction of the dam was completed in 1963. It took 14 years after its completion for the lake to fill.

Climate

After Nevada, Utah is the second-driest state in the country. Its deserts and lowlands receive little rainfall while other areas receive much more. For instance, the Great Salt Lake Desert receives less than 5 inches (13 cm) per year, while the mountains of the northeast average 50 inches (127 cm). The Wasatch Mountains often receive more than 60 inches (152 cm) of rain per year. Snow is common in the winter except along Utah's southern border and the Great Salt Lake Desert. But in the north, it is an entirely different story. The ski areas near Salt Lake City have been known to receive more than 400 inches (1,000 cm) of snow each season. Some of the tallest mountain peaks even remain covered with snow throughout the summer.

Visitors come from all over the world to ski in Utah. The state's mountains are home to 14 ski resorts.

Not surprisingly, in view of its varied landscapes, Utah has a climate of contrasts. Both the highest and the lowest temperatures ever recorded in the state happened in the same year. On February 1, 1985, the thermometers at Peter's Sink read –69 degrees Fahrenheit (–56 degrees Celsius). Later that year, on July 5, the citizens of Saint George sizzled when the temperature reached 117 °F (47 °C). But these are extremes. Mostly, the people of Utah enjoy weather that is somewhere in between. Average summer temperatures range from 60 °F (15 °C) in the northeast to 84 °F (29 °C) in the southwest. Winter temperatures average 20 °F (–7 °C) in the north and 39 °F (4 °C) in the south.

Plant Life

With such varied terrain, Utah is home to many types of trees and other plants. Some of these plants have special characteristics that enable them to thrive in the state's often harsh landscapes and high elevations. Juniper and sagebrush can be found in the Sonoran Desert. Wildflowers and meadow grasses thrive at higher elevations. In spring, flowering plants show their colors as they bloom throughout the state. Beavertail cacti distinguish themselves with showy red or purple petals. White sprays of dwarf bearclaw poppies cling to rocks, and purple lupine sway in the breeze.

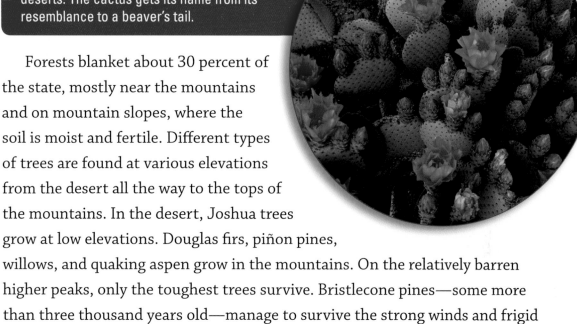

The beavertail cactus can be found in Utah's deserts. The cactus gets its name from its resemblance to a beaver's tail.

Forests blanket about 30 percent of the state, mostly near the mountains and on mountain slopes, where the soil is moist and fertile. Different types of trees are found at various elevations from the desert all the way to the tops of the mountains. In the desert, Joshua trees grow at low elevations. Douglas firs, piñon pines, willows, and quaking aspen grow in the mountains. On the relatively barren higher peaks, only the toughest trees survive. Bristlecone pines—some more than three thousand years old—manage to survive the strong winds and frigid cold temperatures year after year.

Animal Life

While perhaps appearing barren at first glance, Utah's deserts and other dry regions are actually home to several members of the animal kingdom. Poisonous scorpions live mostly under rocks. Scorpions and their ancestors have lived in Utah for more than 400 million years. Reptiles such as rattlesnakes, lizards, and tortoises inhabit the state's dry regions. Desert horned lizards—sometimes called horned toads—live in the sandy areas of western Utah. Small mammals such as the desert shrew thrive in the dry and warm climate. Desert shrews are typically found in the southwestern part of the state.

Across Utah's grasslands, badgers shovel their way into the dirt, searching for a cool place to call home. With their strong legs, badgers can dig faster than humans. Coyotes can be found in the grasslands, forests, and other habitats. They typically travel alone, constantly on the lookout for jackrabbits and small rodents.

Mule deer, named for their mule-like ears, can be found throughout the state.

Utah's bodies of water are also home to a variety of wildlife. Fish such as trout, perch, carp, and bass live in the state's more than 11,000 miles (17,700 km) of streams and 147,000 acres (59,500 ha) of reservoirs and lakes. Frogs, salamanders, and other amphibians live in or near these bodies of water. Geese, mallard ducks, avocets, American white pelicans, and herons are some of the many birds that seek out the state's waters.

Birds soar through the skies above Utah. Golden eagles, hawks, sparrows, wrens, chickadees, ravens, woodpeckers, owls, and swallows are also among Utah's many feathered residents.

Utah's forests are filled with animals, including black bears, raccoons, bats, and squirrels. In the mountains, elk, mule deer, mountain goats, and pronghorn graze on grasses and other plants. Rocky Mountain bighorn sheep are a common sight along the mountain slopes.

Endangered Wildlife

Utah has several species of plants and animals that are considered endangered. An endangered species is at risk of becoming extinct, or completely dying out. Human settlement, overhunting, pesticides, and pollution are some factors that threaten wildlife. Some of the state's endangered birds include the Mexican spotted owl and the whooping crane.

Another threatened species is the Utah prairie dog. It is one of several types of prairie dogs in the state. These rodents make warning sounds that resemble a dog's bark. They can grow to be anywhere from 12 to 20 inches (30 to 50 cm) long, and they live together in underground burrows beneath grassy regions. During the day, these brown rodents come above ground to eat plants and insects. Gunnison's prairie dogs can be found in the southeast, white-tailed prairie dogs live in the northeast, and Utah prairie dogs live in the southwest.

Utah prairie dogs do not live in any other part of the world. Predators, disease, drought, and poisons have contributed to their decline in the past. Thanks to conservation efforts, however, their numbers are on the rebound. In September 2010, the U.S. Fish and Wildlife Service announced a new plan that would continue to help Utah prairie dogs.

More than 100,000 Utah prairie dogs once lived in the wild. Today, that number has been reduced to fewer than 10,000.

Plants & Animals

Indian Paintbrush

This native plant sports a wide range of colors—yellow, red, orange, or cream. It grows best in sandy soils and usually blooms from March through May. Some types of Indian paintbrush are parasitic, meaning they live on other plants. These flowers tap into the roots of other plants and suck out the nutrients they need to grow.

Mule Deer

Mule deer get their name from their large, mule-like ears. The large ears flick about, trying to pick up the faint sound of approaching danger. These deer spend the warm months grazing in the mountains, but they move to lower elevations during the snowy winters.

Desert Bighorn Sheep

This sure-footed mammal prefers dry rocky areas and is a master cliff-climber. Bighorn sheep usually live in groups, grazing on grasses and bushes during the day. In autumn, these animals move to the valleys. They return to the high mountain pastures when the snow has melted in the spring.

Beavertail Cactus

Beavertail cacti can be found on the dry, rocky desert slopes of southwestern Utah. They get their name from their shape—flat and rounded, just like a beaver's tail. Bright red or lavender blooms sprout from this prickly plant from March through June. The cacti are low-growing and spread easily, inching across the desert floor.

Desert Tortoise

Desert tortoises live off wildflowers and dried plants and grasses. Because of disease and the habitat loss, the desert tortoise population is very low. In Utah, these reptiles are a threatened species, which means they are at risk of becoming endangered. Efforts are being made to try to increase the state's tortoise population.

Mojave Desert Sidewinder

This snake slides through the dry deserts, sand dunes, and rocky hillsides of Utah. It winds its way among low shrubs in its search for lizards, kangaroo rats, and any other rodent that crosses its path. As its name implies, it moves itself sideways, by forming S-shaped curves with its body.

From the Beginning

The first humans to live in what is now Utah are believed to have arrived about 11,000 years ago. These early people were known as Paleo-Indians. Experts believe that they were descendants of people who came to North America using a natural land bridge that once connected Alaska and Asia. From there, these early people moved throughout North America.

The Paleo-Indians were nomadic. They traveled from place to place, hunting and gathering food. They lived off the region's abundant wildlife. Paleo-Indians used spears tipped with rock to hunt giant prehistoric animals, such as woolly mammoths.

A new group of ancient people—the Desert Archaic—inhabited the area about 8,000 years ago. At that time, people lived in simple settlements, either in small villages or in cave dwellings. Danger Cave and Juke Box Cave, both near Wendover, are two areas known to have been occupied at that time.

About 2,500 years ago, agriculture became much more important to the inhabitants of the area. People planted corn, beans, and squash in the region's fertile valleys. In the Four Corners area, a people known today as the Ancestral Puebloans grew their own food and built their own cliff dwellings. These cliff

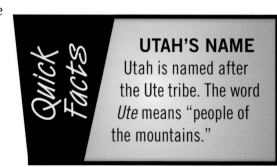

Quick Facts

UTAH'S NAME
Utah is named after the Ute tribe. The word *Ute* means "people of the mountains."

Cliff dwellings built by the Ancestral Puebloans can be seen in the Grand Gulch Primitive Area.

dwellings, called pueblos, were made of adobe (mud) and built into canyon walls.

By 500 CE, a new group—the Fremont—had moved into the region. They were hunters and gatherers. They lived in pit houses—large hollows dug out of the ground. The Fremont left traces of their culture across Utah. Remains of their dwellings have been found throughout the state. Archaeologists have also discovered remnants of Fremont and Ancestral Puebloan tools, baskets, pottery, and clay figurines.

The Fremont also carved pictures on rock walls in the region. These rock carvings are called petroglyphs. They include animal shapes, as well as large human figures that have triangle-shaped shoulders and wear elaborate necklaces. Examples of these petroglyphs can be seen at the Fremont Indian State Park in Sevier. The park spans more than 1,000 acres (400 ha) and includes a visitor center, museum, and areas for camping, fishing, picnicking, and hiking.

Indians of the More Recent Past

After 1300, other American Indian groups sought out the area as well. The Ute, the Southern Paiute, the Navajo, the Goshute (or Gosiute), and the Northern and Eastern Shoshone all made the region their home. They hunted, fished, and gathered wild plants. The piñon nut, the fruit of a type of pine tree, became a popular treat. Groups of women, especially Paiute and Navajo, often trekked into the dry stretches of Utah countryside to gather the tiny nuts in baskets. Beginning in the 1600s, the Navajo in the Four Corners region herded sheep, goats, and cattle. They became known for their skill as weavers, making beautiful wool blankets with complex designs.

UTAH'S PREHISTORIC PAST

Many millions of years ago, dinosaurs roamed through leafy forests in the land that is now Utah. Fossils from this prehistoric period have been preserved at sites and museums throughout the state. The remains of hundreds of fossilized dinosaur bones are embedded in a cliff wall inside "The Quarry" at Dinosaur National Monument, located near Vernal, Utah.

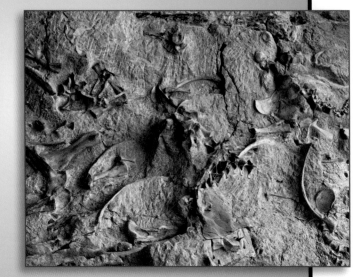

Utah's native peoples lived in a variety of types of homes. Shelters made out of brush and cone-shaped tepees made from animal hides dotted the landscape. The Ute brought the tepee to Utah. It was a style they borrowed from the Indians who lived on the Great Plains. The Southern Paiute made rounded houses, called wickiups, which were formed by carefully arranging brush and poles. Some groups, such as the Goshute, moved from place to place, so they often searched for simple shelters. They gathered in caves or learned to make a short-term home out of the cracks and crevices in the landscape.

Although there were many different groups of people in the region, most American Indians lived in peace. The Ute were known to be raiders and warriors, however. They searched out prosperous settlements and forced the people there to share their wealth. They also became skilled buffalo hunters, bearing down on these huge animals on their swift horses. The Ute and other groups began using horses after the Spanish brought the animals to the Americas in the 1500s. Horses changed life for Ute and other American Indian groups. On horseback, American Indians could more easily hunt large game, attack neighboring villages, or travel great distances.

MAKING PETROGLYPHS

A petroglyph is a picture carved into stone using tools. You can make your own petroglyphs similar to the ones the Fremont people made more than a thousand years ago.

WHAT YOU NEED

Aluminum foil, waxed paper, or plastic sheet

$^1/_2$ cup (75 grams) of low-fire potter's clay
(available in art supply stores)

Empty straight-sided jar or rolling pin

Large nail

Newspaper

Plastic knife or clay tools

Two short pieces of cord,
each about 6 inches (15 cm) long

Spread out the foil, waxed paper, or plastic sheet on your workspace.

Knead the clay for a few minutes to help prevent cracking. Form the clay into two balls. Roll the jar or rolling pin over each ball until the clay flattens into a disk as thin as two or three quarters stacked on top of one another.

Near the edge of each disk, use the nail to make a hole straight through the disk. Set the clay on the newspaper to begin drying.

Twelve to twenty-four hours later, scratch a design into each clay disk with the nail, plastic knife, or clay tools. (If you wait longer, the clay is more likely to crack when you do this.) You might draw a person or animal like those on Fremont petroglyphs. You can also create your own symbols and drawings.

Let each disk dry completely. String the cord through the hole to hang it.

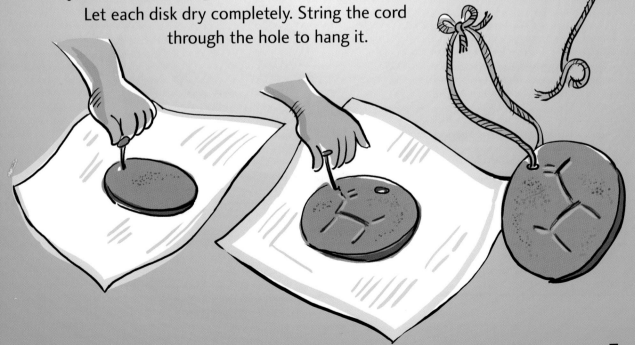

Explorers, Trappers, and Traders

During the mid-1700s, Spanish explorers from Mexico traveled through what is now Utah. Juan Maria de Rivera was the first Spanish explorer known to visit the region. Starting in 1765, he led at least two expeditions into what is now Utah. De Rivera and his group reached the Colorado River near present-day Moab in the southeastern part of the state.

More than a decade later, another chapter in European exploration was added. Two Franciscan priests, Francisco Atanasio Domínguez and Silvestre Vélez de Escalante, led a team that left Santa Fe in present-day New Mexico. They hoped to spread Christianity among the American Indians of the region. These explorers also wanted to find an overland route between Santa Fe and California. They entered Utah from the east and trekked through the Uinta Basin, crossing the Wasatch Mountains. They ended up at tribal camps along what is now called Utah Lake, the state's largest freshwater lake. Turning south, they followed the edge of the mountain chain, crossing the Colorado River. But their hopes of reaching Monterey, California, were dashed by fierce blizzards. The group returned to Santa Fe in 1777.

Quick Facts

THE MAN OF THE MOUNTAINS

French-Canadian Étienne Provost was a successful fur trapper and trader who earned the nickname the Man of the Mountains. Several places in central Utah are named after him, including the Provo River, Provo Canyon, and the city of Provo.

Those first steps eventually led to the well-worn paths of settlement. But people of European descent did not begin settling in the region until the next century. By the early 1800s, trade routes had been set up between Santa Fe and the American Indians of north-central Utah. Fur trappers and traders called "mountain men" crisscrossed the region. Spain claimed the region, and then Mexico, after Mexico won its independence from Spain in 1821. People came from all directions, however, including Americans from the east and Canadians from the north. Americans probably first came to the region in 1811 or 1812. Most came in search of the valuable furs of beavers and other fur-bearing animals.

This painting shows fur traders transporting pelts on the Bear River in the 1800s.

By the 1820s, most of Utah had been explored and mapped. One of the most legendary trappers, Jim Bridger, first spotted the Great Salt Lake in 1824. When he tasted its saltiness, he thought it was an ocean. Bridger was one of the mountain men recruited by William H. Ashley's fur-trading company. Ashley hired trappers to work for his company, which was based in St. Louis, Missouri. Each spring, Ashley collected furs from the trappers at a meeting spot along the Green River in Utah.

In the 1840s, an official U.S. government scouting party bound for California passed through Utah. Army engineer John C. Frémont, known as the Pathfinder of the West, mapped countless trails through the land that is now Utah. Fur trapper and frontiersman Kit Carson joined him as a guide on later expeditions. Through written records, Frémont added to the growing knowledge of the area's plant and animal life. His maps helped later pioneers find the fastest and safest routes through Utah.

Mormon Country

For the area's American Indians, after centuries of living in a world without borders, life was about to change. A wave of white settlers eager to head west in search of religious freedom soon poured into the region. This first group to create permanent settlements in Utah was the Mormons.

Mormons belong to The Church of Jesus Christ of Latter-day Saints. This church was founded in New York by Joseph Smith Jr. in 1830. Smith and his followers believed that Christ had returned to Earth to preach among the people. Their beliefs were laid out in The Book of Mormon. But Smith's teachings were unpopular with many people. The Mormons faced violence and mistrust nearly everywhere they went. They were often forced to move from town to town. In June 1844, Smith was killed in Carthage, Illinois, by an angry mob that disagreed with Mormon beliefs.

Leadership of the Mormon church then fell to Brigham Young. He decided to lead his people west in search of a new homeland. Their long, hard journey from Nauvoo, Illinois, by wagon trains began on February 4, 1846. The first group made its way to Nebraska and set up a camp called Winter Quarters, near present-day Omaha, to wait for spring. From Winter Quarters, on April 16, 1847, a scouting party of 148 pioneers set off in search of a new place to settle. The small group included 143 men (three of whom were African American), three women, and two children.

Frémont's maps and reports helped convince the Mormon pioneers that what is now Utah was the place where they would finally find a permanent home. Some of the group entered the Salt Lake Valley on July 22, 1847. Another part of the group, including Young, arrived two days later.

Many others would later join them. A large number of Mormon pioneers made their journey in covered wagons. From 1856 to 1860, others traveled on foot, pushing their household items in handcarts. This period became known as the Handcart Migration. The settlers immediately got to work, building their new society. The pioneers constructed irrigation systems across the desert so they could water crops. In the first few years, life was hard for the Mormons. But this was not the first challenge they had faced. They were armed with determination, a strong group ethic, and of course, their faith. By 1869, about 70,000 Mormon pioneers had trekked across the plains and settled in Utah.

In Their Own Words

"This is the place, drive on."

—Brigham Young, upon arriving in the Salt Lake Valley in 1847

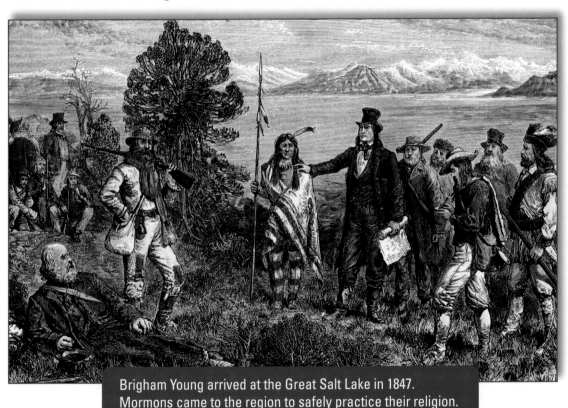

Brigham Young arrived at the Great Salt Lake in 1847. Mormons came to the region to safely practice their religion.

PIONEER DAY

Pioneer Day is a state holiday in Utah. Each year, it is celebrated on July 24th to honor the arrival of Mormon leader Brigham Young and his followers into the Salt Lake Valley in 1847. The day honors the bravery and endurance of the early pioneers.

Young planned for a beautiful city to be built at the northern end of the Salt Lake Valley. It was called Great Salt Lake City. In 1868, "Great" was dropped from the name. The Mormon church's ruling body served as the region's first government. Starting out as a small frontier outpost, Salt Lake City grew into Utah's major urban center.

Salt Lake City serves as the state capital today, and it is home to many historic sites. Young designated the site where Salt Lake Temple would be built.

The Journey's End monument, located in This is the Place State Park, honors Utah's first Mormon pioneers.

The temple was constructed out of Utah granite as the centerpiece of the city's Temple Square. It took forty years to build. Only Mormons can enter Salt Lake Temple. Nearby is the dome-shaped Mormon Tabernacle where the famous Mormon Tabernacle Choir sings. It is known for its huge pipe organ. Also in the area is Young's family home, called the Beehive House.

Success was hard won for Mormons, but soon their ideals and communities spread throughout the region. By 1900, the group had established more than five hundred settlements in Utah and in its neighboring regions. Missionaries recruited new members, so even more settlers continued to seek out the open space of the West.

Utah Territory

When Brigham Young and his group of settlers arrived in the Salt Lake Valley in 1847, what is now Utah still belonged to Mexico. However, when the Mexican-American War ended in 1848, the United States gained the rights to a huge area of land under the Treaty of Guadalupe Hidalgo. That land included present-day Utah. After the war, even more people entered the region. As a result, the following years were often a time of struggle and debate. Who would be in charge of the future state? In 1850, the Mormons sent a petition to the U.S. government requesting that their land be recognized as the territory of Deseret. The government denied their request. Instead, it created a territory called Utah.

The territory's first capital city was Fillmore. Located near the center of the present-day state, it was named in honor of President Millard Fillmore. Brigham Young served as the territory's first governor. The U.S. government was fearful, however, of Mormons running the newly created Utah Territory. Who would control its vast resources?

Meanwhile, American Indians claimed the land the newcomers wanted for their own. As a result, tensions between the settlers and American Indians grew. Treaties and promises between the two groups were often broken, and land promised to the Indians was taken away. As many of their game animals were killed or driven away by the settlers, Indians also faced starvation. Some were forced to raid villages and settlements to seek food. Many American Indians also died from diseases brought by the settlers. Eventually, wars broke out between settlers and Indians. The Walker War extended over a two-year period starting in 1853. American Indians killed a team sent by the U.S. government to survey the land in 1854. They raided settlements and attacked stagecoach stations.

In 1857, during what became known as the Utah War, an event occurred that is now called the Mountain Meadow Massacre. President James Buchanan wished to reduce the power of Brigham Young and his thousands of Mormons in the territory. He appointed a new governor, Alfred Cumming of Georgia, and sent forces west to back up the order. Before they could arrive, a party of about 140 travelers was passing through Utah on its way to California. Some members of this group were thought to be opposed to Mormons. Angry and threatened, a group of Mormons and their Indian allies attacked the travelers, killing nearly the entire party. Mormon leader John D. Lee was put on trial and executed for his role in the attack.

From 1865 to 1872, a series of battles took place between Ute and white settlers. Joined by other tribes, the Ute were led by chief Antonga Black Hawk. The conflict became known as the Black Hawk War. After seven years of struggle, the Ute were seriously weakened and forced to live on reservations.

The Battle of Bad Axe was the final conflict of the Black Hawk War.

The Road to Statehood

Thanks to new developments in communications and transportation, Utah's isolation was about to end. On October 24, 1861, the country's first transcontinental telegraph system connecting Washington, D.C., and San Francisco was completed in Salt Lake City. With a quick click of the keys, telegraph operators could send messages from both coasts to Utah.

Next, the railroad came roaring into Utah. On May 10, 1869, after several years of difficult construction work, two railroad lines—the Union Pacific and the Central Pacific—finally met at Promontory Summit in Utah. The meeting marked the completion of the first

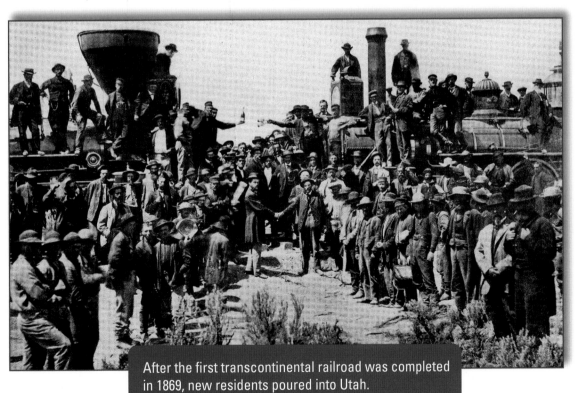

After the first transcontinental railroad was completed in 1869, new residents poured into Utah.

BUTCH CASSIDY

Butch Cassidy was born Robert LeRoy Parker in Beaver, Utah, in the late 1860s. With the help of his sidekick, the Sundance Kid, and the Wild Bunch Gang, Cassidy staged a series of daring train, bank, and mine-payroll robberies starting in 1896. By the end of the 1800s, his gang had the longest streak of successful bank robberies in the history of the West. In the early 1900s, Cassidy and the Sundance Kid went to South America, where they may have been killed by Bolivian soldiers in 1908. The popular 1969 movie *Butch Cassidy and the Sundance Kid* was based on the outlaws' lives.

transcontinental railroad in the United States. The railroad connected east to west. To celebrate the joining of the railroad at Promontory Summit, excited crowds gathered for the hammering of the last railroad spike. Called the Golden Spike, it was actually made of gold.

The main railroad line soon branched off, connecting formerly remote towns. For many settlers, the years of isolation were over. The railroad also meant a flood of new faces. Non-Mormons poured into Utah, bringing varied cultures and religions. Many came to seek their fortune in the state's mining boom. Coal, gold, silver, lead, and copper were being mined. By the 1870s, the large mining industry helped bring wealth to the region.

From 1860 to 1890, Utah's population soared from 40,000 to more than 200,000 residents. Valleys in the Wasatch Mountains and parts of southern Utah gave rise to cities and towns. Despite the rapid changes, the Mormon way of life still dominated the region. The Mormons argued that under their steady guidance the territory had grown. But Mormon control over local and territorial governments continued to be challenged, in part because certain Mormon practices were in conflict with federal law. Finally, after a long struggle for statehood, a state constitution completely consistent with federal law was adopted at a constitutional convention in 1895. On January 4, 1896, Utah was admitted to the Union as the forty-fifth state.

Thanks to the mining industry, Salt Lake City thrived in the early 1900s.

A New Century

The twentieth century saw even more rapid growth. Urban centers continued to develop and spread. Railroads and improved roads meant new markets for Utah's ranchers and farmers. Ranchers increased the size of their herds, as raising sheep and beef cattle grew in importance. At the same time, the federal government funded a project that channeled water from the Strawberry River to nearby farmland. The project was finished in 1913 and improved irrigation to some of the state's drier patches.

But it was mining that became Utah's strongest industry. In the nineteenth century, silver was king, but by the twentieth century, copper mining had taken the lead. Mining techniques and technology improved. Surface mining was introduced at Utah's Bingham Canyon in 1906. The smelting industry also met with success. Starting in the early 1900s, large smelters were built in the Salt Lake Valley. They melted and refined the metals taken from the mines. During World War I, in which the United States fought from 1917 to 1918, Utah was ready to meet the nation's growing need for metals.

The Great Depression, which began in 1929, was a time of economic hardship for the entire country. Many businesses failed, and people found themselves out of work. Utah was hit especially hard. Many who worked in Utah's mining and agricultural industries lost their jobs. With more than one in three people in Utah unemployed, families struggled through those tough years.

It was not until World War II, in which the United States fought

> # *In Their Own Words*
>
> *Here in Utah, I've always received a ton of support. They really make me feel at home here.... The Olympic spirit is always in the air here.*
>
> —Apolo Anton Ohno, Olympic gold medalist in short-track speed skating, who competed in the 2002 Winter Olympics in Salt Lake City

from 1941 to 1945, that the economy rebounded. The need for steel and other war-related supplies from mines and factories provided many jobs for Utahns. Increased demand for food to feed troops boosted Utah's agricultural industry. In addition, Hill Air Force Base in northern Utah became a key military supply center, employing thousands.

The second half of the twentieth century saw even greater shifts. Utah's economy was forced to change again. Mining and agriculture declined in the state. In its place tourism boomed. People came from all over to visit Utah's beautiful landscape and learn about its history.

In 2002, Salt Lake City hosted the nineteenth Winter Olympic Games. The Games drew thousands of people to the city, and millions more learned about the city and state through media coverage of the Olympics and its venues. Visitors and viewers had the opportunity to see the state's natural beauty and better understand the sense of the history and heritage that makes Utah unique.

Speed skater Apolo Ohno became a household name after winning a gold medal and a silver medal at the 2002 Winter Olympic Games.

UTAH JAZZ

The 2002 Winter Olympics may be long over, but Utah's passion for sports continues. Salt Lake City is home to the National Basketball Association's Utah Jazz. In the 1980s and 1990s, the Jazz roster included future Hall of Famers Karl Malone and John Stockton. The duo was one of the most celebrated in basketball history. Malone finished second on the all-time career points list (36,928). Stockton finished first all-time in assists (15,806).

Important Dates

★ **1300** The Ute, Paiute, Goshute, Shoshone, and Navajo peoples inhabit parts of present-day Utah.

★ **1765** Spaniard Juan Maria Antonio de Rivera is the first European known to set foot in what is now Utah.

★ **1776** Spanish missionaries Silvestre Vélez de Escalante and Francisco Atanasio Domínguez seek a new route from New Mexico to California via Utah.

★ **1824** Fur trapper Jim Bridger reaches the Great Salt Lake.

★ **1843** John C. Frémont begins exploring the Great Salt Lake region.

★ **1847** Brigham Young and the first group of Mormon settlers arrive in the Salt Lake Valley.

★ **1848** Utah becomes part of the United States after the Mexican-American War.

★ **1850** The U.S. government establishes the Utah Territory.

★ **1856–1860** Three thousand Mormons relocate to Utah in what is known as the Handcart Migration.

★ **1857–1858** Brigham Young is removed as territorial governor by President James Buchanan. More than two thousand soldiers accompany the new governor, setting off the Utah War.

★ **1865–1872** The Black Hawk War becomes the last major American Indian conflict in Utah.

★ **1869** The first transcontinental railroad is completed at Promontory Summit, Utah.

★ **1896** Utah becomes the forty-fifth state on January 4.

★ **1964** Arizona's Glen Canyon Dam on the Colorado River creates Lake Powell, the nation's second-largest artificial lake. Much of Lake Powell is in Utah.

★ **1999** A rare tornado tears through downtown Salt Lake City on August 11, causing more than $100 million in damage.

★ **2002** Salt Lake City hosts the nineteenth Winter Olympic Games.

★ **2010** Scientists discover fossils of two new plant-eating dinosaur species closely related to Triceratops, including one with fifteen horns on its head.

The People

Utah is one of the fastest-growing states in the country. Still, vast stretches of the state remain uninhabited, and two-thirds of all U.S. states have larger populations than Utah does. About three times as many people live in New York City as reside in Utah. Most of Utah's 2.8 million residents live in cities and towns along Wasatch Front in the Salt Lake City area. The Wasatch Front is located on the western side of the Wasatch Mountains. The state's largest and most populated city is its capital, Salt Lake City, with more than 186,000 residents. Other Utah cities with populations over 100,000 are West Valley City, Provo, and West Jordan.

Although Utah is only the thirty-fourth most populous state, it is home to people of diverse ethnic and racial backgrounds. Hispanic Americans are the largest minority group. African Americans and Asian Americans account for fairly small proportions of the population. About 86 percent of Utahns are white. Among Utahns of European heritage, people of English ancestry make up the largest group. People of Scandinavian and German origin rank second and third.

Mormons made up a large majority of the population during the 1800s. The growth of remote mining towns, however, added diversity to the state. Early in the 1900s, coal mining camps, mostly in Carbon County, sprang up. They were home to miners who had arrived from a variety of far-away places, including Japan, Germany, Poland, the Balkans region of southeastern Europe, Austria,

The majority of Utah's population is white, but the state is home to people of many different racial backgrounds.

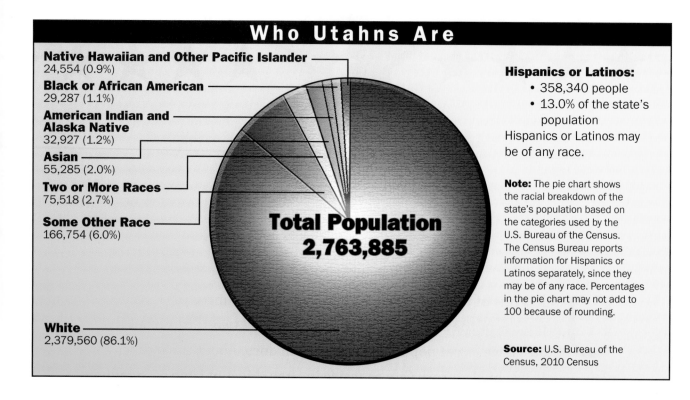

Who Utahns Are

Native Hawaiian and Other Pacific Islander
24,554 (0.9%)

Black or African American
29,287 (1.1%)

American Indian and Alaska Native
32,927 (1.2%)

Asian
55,285 (2.0%)

Two or More Races
75,518 (2.7%)

Some Other Race
166,754 (6.0%)

White
2,379,560 (86.1%)

Total Population 2,763,885

Hispanics or Latinos:
- 358,340 people
- 13.0% of the state's population

Hispanics or Latinos may be of any race.

Note: The pie chart shows the racial breakdown of the state's population based on the categories used by the U.S. Bureau of the Census. The Census Bureau reports information for Hispanics or Latinos separately, since they may be of any race. Percentages in the pie chart may not add to 100 because of rounding.

Source: U.S. Bureau of the Census, 2010 Census

Italy, Greece, Armenia, and Syria. While most of the rest of Utah was Mormon, new arrivals were slowly changing the face of the state. This was the beginning of a trend that has continued. Today, Mormons make up about 60 percent of Utah's population. This percentage is much higher than any other state in the country.

Hispanic Americans

Utah's Hispanic population continues to grow. In the year 2000, 9 percent of the population was of Hispanic origin. A decade later, 13 percent of the population was Hispanic. About three-quarters of Hispanic Americans in Utah are people of Mexican heritage.

The growth of the cattle, sheep, and mining industries first drew Hispanic settlers arriving from across the Southwest. In the early 1900s, immigrants, mostly from Colorado and New Mexico, started settling in southern Utah. Workers from Mexico, who were already living in the area, headed to the north. Hispanics continued to move to Utah in small numbers. The need for labor

More than 9 percent of Utah's families speak Spanish at home.

during World War II contributed to the rise in the Hispanic population, and people of Hispanic origin have continued to seek job opportunities in Utah since then.

American Indians

In 1980, about 19,200 American Indians lived in Utah. This number almost matched the population of about 20,000 Indians living in the area when the Mormons first arrived. Today, about 33,000 American Indians live in the Beehive State. They mostly live and work in urban areas. Others still choose to make their homes on Utah's many reservations, where they feel close ties to their native heritage.

There are more Navajo in Utah than any other Indian group. As of 2000, there were 14,000 living in Utah. During the 2002 Winter Olympics, Navajo officials set up an 11,000-square-foot (28,300-sq-km) hogan, a traditional home, in Salt Lake City. They used the hogan to educate visitors about their nation. Inside there was storytelling, food, and art.

Quick Facts

NAVAJO CODE TALKERS
During World War II, a group of Navajo served as U.S. Marines in the Pacific theater of the war, where the United States was fighting against Japan. The Navajo sent and received top secret messages using a code based on the complex Athapaskan language spoken by many Navajo but by very few other people. It was a code that the Japanese could not break. The Navajo "code talkers," as they were called, included members of Utah's Navajo. Their unbreakable code saved thousands of lives and helped to end the war.

FROM HAWAII TO UTAH

In 1889, forty-six Hawaiians and Polynesians founded the town of Iosepa in Skull Valley, southwest of Salt Lake City. Iosepa is Hawaiian for Joseph. The town was named after Joseph F. Smith, one of the first missionaries to visit the Hawaiian Islands and the sixth president of the Mormon Church. The town grew, and over the next twenty-eight years, more Mormon converts arrived. In 1917, the last residents left and moved to a new Mormon plantation back in Hawaii.

The Mormon Majority

The worldwide headquarters for the Mormon Church has been located in Salt Lake City since Mormon pioneers first settled there in 1847, and Mormons still make up a majority of Utah's population. The Mormon Church is the sixth-largest religion in the United States. It runs missionary programs that draw new members all the time. Young men are called on to spend two years spreading the faith either in the United States or in a foreign nation. Most usually leave for their missions after graduating from high school or after a year of college. After their missions, most return to complete their college education. Young women may also serve missions after

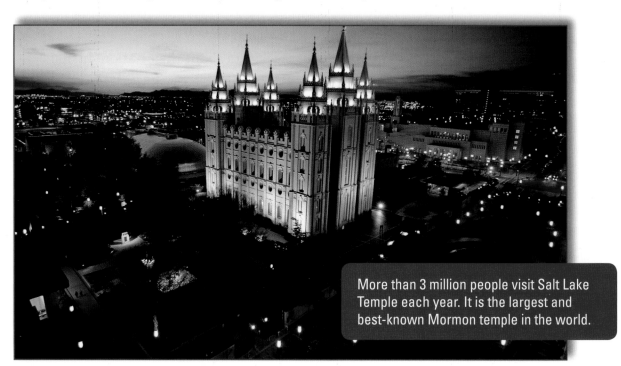

More than 3 million people visit Salt Lake Temple each year. It is the largest and best-known Mormon temple in the world.

The Mormon Tabernacle Choir, which began in the mid-1800s, is made up of 360 men and women. The choir has won Grammy and Emmy awards.

they reach the age of twenty-one. Many people who move to Utah come as a result of this missionary effort. They wish to be closer to Mormon communities and Mormon ideals.

Another reason for the large Mormon population in the state is family size. In general, Mormon families tend to have more children than the national average. It is not surprising, then, that Utah has the highest birthrate and the largest average family size in the nation. The state has more than twenty live births per thousand residents, compared to about fourteen for the nation as a whole. Utah also has the country's youngest population. Family life is a central part of the Mormon faith.

In March 2002, officials announced that the church no longer wished to be called simply the Mormon Church or the Latter-day Saints Church. They said they wanted the full name of the church—The Church of Jesus Christ of Latter-day Saints—to be used when referring to their religion. They still wanted to be called Mormons but feared they were being viewed not as a religious community, but as an ethnic or cultural group. Church officials wanted to change any notion that Mormonism has little to do with Christianity. By emphasizing the church's full name, they hoped to make their connection to other Christians clearer.

Famous Utahns

Brigham Young: Religious Leader

Young, born in Vermont in 1801, led the first band of Mormon settlers to Utah in 1847. He founded Salt Lake City and helped establish more than three hundred other Mormon towns. Young was Utah's first territorial governor, serving from 1850 to 1857. He was president of The Church of Jesus Christ of Latter-day Saints until his death in 1877. Brigham Young University is named after him.

J. Willard Marriott: Businessman

In 1900, Marriott was born in Marriott Settlement near Ogden. He founded the now-famous worldwide hotel chain that bears his name in 1957. Claiming "the answer to most obstacles lies in persistence, hard work, and faith in self," Marriott grew his company into a multibillion-dollar business by the time he died in 1985.

Philo T. Farnsworth: Inventor

Farnsworth was born near Beaver in 1906. His name might not be well-known, but his invention surely is. By the time he was twenty-one, Farnsworth had produced and patented the first electronic television system. His work also paved the way for such developments as radar, electron microscopes, and systems to guide airplanes. He died in 1971.

Nolan Bushnell: Video Game Pioneer

Born in Clearfield in 1943, Nolan Bushnell is considered one of the founding fathers of the video game industry. In the early 1970s, he invented Pong, one of the world's first video games. He also co-founded Atari, one of the first major video game makers. In the late 1970s, Bushnell started the Chuck E. Cheese's entertainment centers as places where kids could go to eat pizza and play video games.

Donny and Marie Osmond: Entertainers

Brother-and-sister singing act Donny (born in 1957) and Marie (born in 1959) are natives of Ogden. In 1976, they made television history by becoming the youngest hosts of a prime-time program, *The Donny & Marie Show*. In recent years, they have continued to perform in shows, including in Las Vegas and on Broadway in New York City. Both siblings have competed on *Dancing with the Stars*.

Steve Young: Football Player

A direct descendant of Brigham Young, quarterback Steve Young was born in Salt Lake City in 1961. His family moved to Connecticut when he was in elementary school. Young returned to Utah to attend Brigham Young University (BYU). He played football for BYU, but he is best known for his years with the San Francisco 49ers. In January 1995, he led the 49ers to the Super Bowl championship. Young was inducted into the Pro Football Hall of Fame in 2005.

A Fast-Growing State

According to the U.S. Census Bureau, Utah's population increased by more than 530,000 people from 2000 to 2010. This growth rate of almost 24 percent made Utah the third-fastest-growing state in the first decade of the twenty-first century, after Nevada and Arizona. High birth rates, low death rates, and a continued influx of people looking for job opportunities have all contributed to the growth.

Utah faces challenges from the rapid growth of its urban centers. States such as Utah, once known for their wide-open spaces, are experiencing an encroachment on these lands. Other problems include overcrowding and increased traffic in cities and their surrounding suburbs. For years, many Utahns thought their state would be free from urban sprawl, but now they see increased numbers of strip malls, housing developments, and superhighways common to large urban areas.

Education

Education is important to the people of Utah—and a challenge at the same time. Since Utah has the country's highest birthrate, the proportion of school-age children in the state is high. Almost one-third of Utahns are under 18 years old, compared to less than one-fourth for the nation as a whole. That means the state has to find ways to efficiently use tax dollars that are spent on education.

On average, Utahns tend to be highly educated. Almost nine out of ten adults in the state have graduated from high school, and more than a quarter have

More than 95 percent of Brigham Young University students are Mormon.

graduated from college. Both figures are higher than the national average. Utah has also had one of the highest literacy rates in the United States.

Utah is home to several colleges and universities. The first was the University of Deseret. It was established in 1850 and later renamed the University of Utah. Located in Salt Lake City, the University of Utah is a public university with about 29,000 students. Founded in 1875, Brigham Young University is located in Provo. The Mormon Church owns the university. About 34,000 students attend BYU.

STEPHENIE MEYER

World-famous author Stephenie Meyer graduated from Brigham Young University with a degree in English. A member of The Church of Jesus Christ of Latter-day Saints, Meyer says her beliefs have influenced her writing. The novels in her Twilight Saga have sold millions of copies around the world and have all been made into popular movies.

★ Sundance Film Festival

Each January, budding filmmakers from across the country compete for top prizes and the opportunity to have their films viewed around the world. Hollywood actor and director Robert Redford founded this film festival in Park City in 1981. The once-small festival has grown into a media extravaganza. Each year, thousands of filmmakers and movie fans flock to the festival to see the premieres of independent films that may become famous.

★ Bryce Canyon Winter Festival

Bryce Canyon is known for its amazing rock formations called hoodoos. The Bryce Canyon area gets its share of snow. So what better way to celebrate than with all the great winter activities the area offers? This annual February event features cross-country ski races, snow-sculpting contests, ski archery competitions, photography workshops, and live entertainment in the evenings.

★ Utah Summer Games

The Utah Summer Games in Cedar City is an annual Olympic-style sports festival for amateur athletes in Utah. This June event showcases about 9,600 amateur athletes who have qualified in regional competitions held across the state. About 50,000 spectators enjoy watching the various events.

★ Utah Arts Festival

Each June, the arts take center stage in Salt Lake City. From the culinary to the visual to the performing arts, artists of all sorts fill the streets of the state's capital to put their vision and creations on display.

★ Days of '47

This July celebration honors the state's early settlers who first arrived in 1847. The month is filled with activities in Salt Lake City, including parades, concerts, fireworks displays, and a rodeo. It all leads up to Pioneer Day on July 24. This day is marked by one of the largest and oldest parades in the United States.

★ Western Legends Roundup

Cowboy poets, musicians, and storytellers converge on Kanab each summer. The celebration captures the spirit and flavor of the Old West. Festivalgoers can also sample authentic Western food and visit the sets and backdrops that have been featured in countless films.

★ Moab Music Festival

Started in 1992, this annual September event offers instrumental and vocal music programs in the beautiful red-rock region of southeastern Utah. The festival provides a full schedule of concerts. It also brings local students in touch with world-class musicians.

★ Utah State Fair

The Utah State Fair is held each September in Salt Lake City. This exciting celebration features a music competition, a rodeo, carnival games, animal displays, fireworks, and top national musical acts.

How the Government Works

Utah is still run under the constitution that was adopted in 1895, just before it became a state. A state constitution describes how a state's government is organized and what powers the government has. A state constitution also sets limits on the powers of government, in order to protect the rights of individuals. The Utah constitution divides the state government into three separate branches. The executive branch administers state laws, the legislative branch makes new laws or changes existing ones, and the judicial branch interprets laws.

Like all states, Utah is represented in the U.S. Congress in Washington, D.C. Each state elects two U.S. senators, who serve six-year terms. There is no limit on the number of terms a U.S. senator can serve. A state's population determines the number of people that it sends to the U.S. House of Representatives. Beginning

Quick Facts

WOMEN'S SUFFRAGE
Women nationwide did not have the right to vote in elections until the Nineteenth Amendment to the U.S. Constitution went into effect in 1920. However, suffragists (people who supported voting rights for women) in Utah worked hard to make the state one of the first in the country to allow women to vote in state and local elections. Utah's constitution granted women the right to vote in those elections, beginning in 1896.

The State Capitol building, in Salt Lake City, was completed in 1916.

Branches of Government

EXECUTIVE ★ ★ ★ ★ ★ ★ ★ ★

The governor heads the executive branch. Utah's voters elect the governor to a four-year term. There is no limit on the number of terms the governor can serve. The governor prepares budgets and oversees certain areas of state business, such as tax policies and education. Other executive branch officials include the attorney general, lieutenant governor, state auditor, and state treasurer.

LEGISLATIVE ★ ★ ★ ★ ★ ★ ★ ★

Utah's legislature consists of two parts, or chambers. There is a senate with twenty-nine senators who serve four-year terms and a house of representatives with seventy-five members who serve two-year terms. There is no limit on the number of terms that state legislators may serve.

JUDICIAL ★ ★ ★ ★ ★ ★ ★ ★

Utah has different courts that make up the judicial branch. The state supreme court is the state's highest judicial body. It is made up of five justices who serve ten-year, renewable terms. Utah's court of appeals has seven justices who serve six-year, renewable terms. In addition, each of the state's eight judicial districts has one or more judges. Juvenile and municipal courts also serve the public.

in 2013, Utah will have four representatives in the House. This is an increase of one seat because of the size of Utah's population growth in the first decade of the twenty-first century. U.S. House members serve two-year terms and can be reelected an unlimited number of times.

State Government

The state government is responsible for issues that affect the state as a whole. The job of state officials includes drafting, approving, and enforcing laws, as well as managing state budgets. The state government also handles issues between Utah and other states or between Utah and the federal government in Washington, D.C. Utah's state government is centered in the state capital, Salt Lake City.

Local Government

Utah is divided into twenty-nine counties. Most of these counties are managed by a three-person board of county commissioners. Two of the board's members are elected to four-year terms. The third is elected for only two years. That helps encourage change and variety in this very important role. The board of county commissioners is in charge of running the county. This means that it manages a range of services from having snowy roads plowed to approving the purchase of new library books. In a few counties, the executive and legislative branches are separated. A county executive and a separate county council work together to serve local citizens.

Most other county officials serve four-year terms. These officials include attorneys,

Utah's residents may gather at the State Capitol to make their views known on issues they feel strongly about.

Utah's state legislature meets inside the State Capitol building.

treasurers, clerks, auditors, property assessors, and land surveyors. These people all work to improve life on the local level. They also make sure county business runs smoothly.

Utah's towns are free to elect either a mayor or a council—or both—to oversee their affairs. Smaller towns are usually run by a council, which meets from time to time to address the community's concerns. Larger towns often elect both a mayor and a council, while Utah's cities tend to choose commissioners to handle their affairs.

How a Bill Becomes a Law

An idea that eventually becomes a law can be suggested by almost anyone: state officials, the governor, or even state residents. A state legislator then takes the idea and writes a bill, or proposed law, that is submitted to the Office of Legislative Research and General Counsel. The bill is assigned a number and sent to a standing committee of either the senate or house, depending on which chamber of the legislature the member drafting the bill belongs to. In the committee, the strengths and weaknesses of the bill are debated. If a majority of the committee members support the bill, then the entire senate or house can debate it. That way the bill is thrown open to a wider range of opinions. If the first chamber approves the bill, it goes to the other chamber, where the process of considering and voting on the bill is repeated.

Even if the senate and the house both approve a bill, each chamber may have made its own changes, so that their versions of the bill are not exactly the same. In that situation, another committee tries to work out the differences and come up with a final version of the bill that both chambers approve. A final bill, with exactly the same wording, approved by both the house and the senate then goes to the governor. If the governor signs the bill, it becomes law. If the governor disapproves of the bill, he or she can veto, or reject, it. The bill then goes back to the senate and the house. If two-thirds of the members of each house vote to pass the bill, it still becomes law even though the governor had vetoed it.

Utah's lawmakers work to protect and preserve the state's resources and natural beauty.

Sometimes it seems as if important state decisions are made behind closed doors in the state capital. But the door is never shut to the voice of the people. Ideas for new bills often come from everyday citizens. Only by speaking out have some Utahns been able to create change.

The Internet can be the most direct way of contacting local legislators. Utahns can take an active role in government and contact their representative and senator about issues of concern. Legislators serve the people of the state. To contact Utah's state legislators go to

http://le.utah.gov

Click on "Legislator" and "find by address/map." Enter your address or click on the map to look up your senator or representative.

Issues for a New Utah

Elected officials make decisions every day that affect the lives of Utahns. Lawmakers try to serve the people by listening and responding to their needs. Utah now has more people than ever before. With so many residents, there are often disagreements about what is best for the state. Conflicts arise that need solutions. In the twenty-first century, the people of Utah are facing a new set of issues—such as protecting land and other resources, dealing with crowded highways, using limited water supplies effectively to serve a growing population in an arid part of the country, and creating decent jobs.

Making a Living

Some of the major industries that make up Utah's diverse economy include agriculture, mining, and manufacturing. Many businesses in Utah thrive by meeting the needs of tourists and other visitors to the state. Most workers in Utah have jobs in a service industry. Service industry workers help, or provide a service for, people. They are employed in such areas as health care, education, banking and finance, real estate, insurance, software development, restaurants, retail stores, and hotels. About 5 percent of workers in Utah are employed by the government.

Service industries account for the largest portion of the gross state product. The gross state product is the total value of all goods and services produced in the state in a year. Tourism is a major contributor to service industry revenues. Millions of visitors come to explore Utah's beautiful landscape or take part in outdoor recreational activities, such as skiing and hiking.

Quick Facts

NATIONAL PARKS

Tourism is one of Utah's top industries. Many visitors are attracted to the state's five national parks. They include Arches, Bryce Canyon, Canyonlands, Capitol Reef, and Zion. Utah ranks third among all the states in number of national parks. Only Alaska and California have more.

Many Utahns find work in the state's ski resorts, which are usually open from November to May.

No matter what their chosen profession, the people of Utah have a number of options when it comes to looking for work. Despite a rise in unemployment nationally beginning in 2008, Utah remained one of the top states in attracting new businesses and creating jobs. In early 2011, Utah's unemployment rate remained lower than the nationwide figure. Many Utahns also report being very happy with their chosen careers. A survey developed by CareerBliss.com found that employees at Brigham Young University were the third-happiest among workers at all U.S. higher education institutions.

Agriculture

About one-fifth of Utah's land is devoted to farming today. More than 15,000 farms dot the landscape. Utah's major crops include hay, wheat, corn, barley, onions, and potatoes. These crops are mostly grown in the north-central part of the state. Fruits such as apples, peaches, apricots, and cherries are grown in the state's orchards.

Most of Utah's agricultural income—about 70 percent—comes from raising livestock. Just as a century ago, dairy cattle, beef cattle, and sheep remain essential to the state's economy. Most dairy and poultry farms are found east of the Great Salt Lake. Additionally, turkeys and hogs are some of the state's top farm products.

Quick Facts

STATE VEGETABLE
In 2002, elementary school students helped convince the legislature to pass a bill making the Spanish sweet onion Utah's state vegetable. Onion farms cover about 2,500 acres (1,000 ha) in Davis, Weber, and Box Elder counties. These counties grow more than 100 million pounds (45 million kg) of onions each year.

Utah's leading agricultural product is cattle.

RECIPE FOR BEEF JERKY

The beef industry is important to Utah. In parts of Utah, beef jerky is serious business. Some families have even been known to guard their own secret recipes.

WHAT YOU NEED

$1\frac{1}{2}$ to 2 pounds (675 to 900 grams) lean beef (sirloin, top round, or eye round work well)

$\frac{1}{4}$ teaspoon (1 milliliter) pepper

$\frac{1}{4}$ teaspoon (1 ml) garlic powder

$\frac{1}{4}$ cup (60 ml) soy sauce

1 tablespoon (15 ml) Worcestershire sauce

1 teaspoon (5 ml) liquid smoke

Have an adult help you cut the beef into slices that are about $\frac{1}{4}$ to $\frac{1}{2}$ inch (6 to 12 millimeters) thick and 1 to $1\frac{1}{2}$ inches (2.5 to 3.8 cm) wide. Put the strips in a shallow pan.

Combine the five other ingredients. Pour that mixture over the meat. Make sure it spreads to all the pieces of meat. Place the meat in the refrigerator overnight.

With an adult's help, preheat the oven to 150 °F (66 °C). Remove the meat from the refrigerator, and drain the liquid that is left in the pan. Gently dry the strips with paper towel. Place the strips on a cookie sheet, and with an adult's help, put the cookie sheet into the oven. Dry out the beef, until the jerky cracks but does not break if you bend it. Do not try bending the jerky until it is cooled. Once the jerky is done and has cooled, grab a piece and enjoy.

Natural Resources

In the 1800s, Utah's mining industry helped fuel the expansion of railroads. That, in turn, resulted in the economic growth of the state. Today, Utahns still work at a variety of mining-related jobs. Tucked in the Colorado Plateau are some of the state's richest mineral deposits. Near Salt Lake City, Bingham Canyon is known for its veins of copper, silver, gold, and a silvery metal called molybdenum.

The Great Salt Lake is another source of mineral wealth. The lake contains magnesium and several different types of salt. Tin, mercury, lead, uranium, and potassium deposits are also important to the state's mining economy. Clay, limestone, sand, and gravel are other key Utah resources.

Fossil fuels such as coal, petroleum (oil), and natural gas all add to the state's underground wealth. Fossil fuels were formed beneath Earth's surface over millions of years from the remains of prehistoric plants and animals. Petroleum is currently Utah's most valuable mined resource. Most of the state's reserves are located in Duchesne, San Juan, and Uinta counties. Utah's coal is prized for

Quick Facts

BINGHAM CANYON
The Bingham Canyon copper mine in Utah is the biggest human-made hole on Earth. It is more than half a mile (0.8 km) deep and 2.5 miles (4 km) wide.

Workers & Industries

Industry	Number of People Working in That Industry	Percentage of All Workers Who Are Working in That Industry
Education and health care	266,810	21.0%
Wholesale and retail businesses	196,656	15.5%
Publishing, media, entertainment, hotels, and restaurants	139,609	11.0%
Manufacturing	136,210	10.7%
Professionals, scientists, and managers	133,411	10.5%
Construction	94,436	7.4%
Banking and finance, insurance and real estate	89,771	7.1%
Government	68,938	5.4%
Transportation and public utilities	62,653	4.9%
Other services	59,003	4.6%
Farming, forestry, fishing, and mining	24,484	1.9%
Totals	**1,271,981**	**100%**

Notes: Figures above do not include people in the armed forces. "Professionals" includes people such as doctors and lawyers. Percentages may not add to 100 because of rounding.

Source: U.S. Bureau of the Census, 2009 estimates

its low sulfur content. Coal that is low in sulfur can be burned in large quantities without adding a great deal of pollution to the air. Rich deposits are found in Carbon, Emery, and Sevier counties. Large amounts of natural gas come from the southeastern portion of the state.

Manufacturing

Manufacturing was slow to develop in Utah. But with the start of World War II, factories expanded, producing a variety of items. The expansion of factories, in turn, aided the growth of war-related manufacturing. Utah soon became the home of defense plants producing weapons and other materials needed by the military. Over time, steel manufacturing in the state gained a stronger foothold. Provo became the state's leading steel center, due to the rich deposits nearby of limestone, iron, and coal—needed to produce steel.

Today, the value of manufactured products totals about $13 billion annually. Utah is now a center for aerospace research and missile production. Large plants near Brigham City and Salt Lake City produce products such as weapons systems, automobile air bags, and solid rocket propulsion systems for spacecraft.

Film

Filmmakers are drawn to the state's dramatic landscapes. More than fifty feature films have been shot in and around Moab. Kanab, also known as Utah's Little Hollywood, was where more than one hundred classic Westerns were shot. In addition, movie director and actor Robert Redford's Sundance Film Festival in Park City attracts many movie-industry professionals and other visitors to Utah, bolstering the local economy and drawing publicity to the state.

Wheat

In 2009, Utah produced an estimated 7 million bushels (246 million liters) of wheat on 154,000 acres (62,300 ha) of land. The wheat is used for bread, hard rolls, cakes, and pastry flour.

Tourism

Utah is an outdoor-lover's paradise, offering a wide range of activities from skiing to hiking to mountain biking. Each year, millions of visitors pour into the state to get a glimpse of the state's amazing natural beauty.

Coal

Utah is rich in coal reserves. Coal—the state rock—is found in seventeen of Utah's twenty-nine counties. The richest deposits are in Emery and Carbon counties. Utah produces almost 27 million tons (25 million metric tons) per year.

Turkeys

These birds have long been raised in Utah. Sanpete ranks among the top turkey-producing counties in the nation. Statewide, annual turkey production in Utah is around 100 million pounds (45 million kg).

Medical Instruments

Utah manufacturers supply the health-care industry with important medical and dental tools. These tools range from common supplies, such as needles, to complex machines.

High-Tech Industries

The digital age has created a huge demand for new types of products. Utah plants produce computer software and hardware, communications equipment, microchips, and medical and scientific instruments. Novell, a major developer of software, is headquartered in Provo. Businesses have formed the Utah Technology Council. Its goal is to attract high-tech companies to take advantage of the favorable business climate and highly trained workers Utah has to offer.

Protecting the Environment

With a state so rich in natural beauty, it is not surprising that Utahns are concerned about the environment. They share a long history of working to protect their state. Starting in the 1960s, the environment started receiving more attention. At that time, the U.S. Army was testing nerve gas in what engineers thought were barren parts of western Utah. But they were mistaken. About 6,000 sheep were poisoned in the process. This helped to raise the alarm. Utahns got together and called for an end to the storage and testing of such chemicals in the state.

In 1969, the state legislature took the lead in limiting air pollution by implementing stricter regulations on factories. The state continues to be dedicated to decreasing air pollution. Air quality, especially along the Wasatch Front, is continually monitored. In addition, Utah is a member of the Western Regional Air Partnership (WRAP), an alliance of several western states committed to improving air quality.

Some political and business leaders propose using certain desert areas for power plants and mining. They argue that if Utahns develop just a little of their land it will boost the state's economy. But opponents question plans that might yield only short-term results. They are concerned the land will suffer in the long run. The debate continues, with additional plans to use a portion of eastern Utah for petroleum drilling.

In the twenty-first century, Utah continues to develop its mineral wealth. Leaders and citizens hope to limit the harm industry may have on the

Oil is extracted from far below the surface with wells such as this one, in Moab.

Many people come to Utah to enjoy its beautiful scenery.

environment. As Utah's population increases, scientists and government leaders are studying the effect this growth will have. Government officials also keep an eye on Utah's valuable water supplies. They call for smarter water use, recycling, and better ways of disposing of garbage.

The state government stands firmly opposed to having high-level nuclear waste stored within the state's borders. Uranium mills and leaking underground storage tanks are starting to be cleaned up. Preservation of the environment continues to be an utmost concern to state officials and citizens alike.

State Flag & Seal

Adopted in 1913, Utah's flag features the state seal, with the addition of the word **Utah**, *on a field of blue.*

The state seal shows a beehive. Above it is the word **Industry**. *Sego lilies, the state flower, are on either side of the hive, and an American flag is on either side of the lilies. Perched above is an eagle, a symbol of the United States, and six arrows. The seal contains two dates—1847, the year Mormon settlement in Utah began, and 1896, the year Utah was admitted to the Union.*

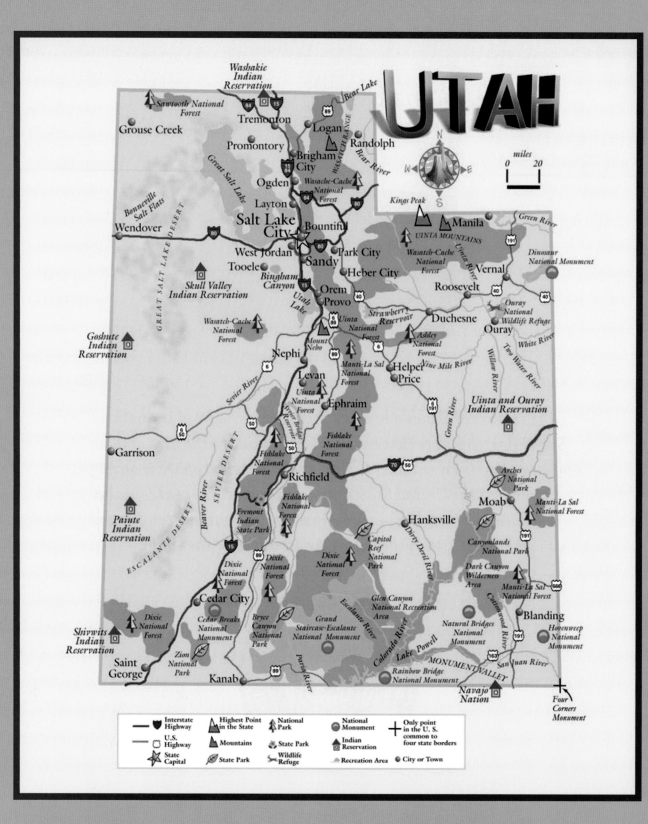

Utah, This Is the Place

words by Sam Francis and Gary Francis
music by Gary Francis

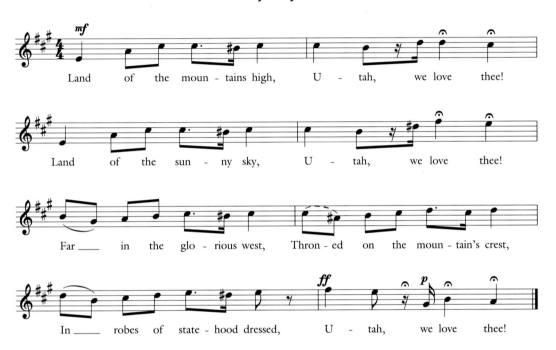

BOOKS

Landau, Elaine. *The Mormon Trail*. Danbury, CT: Children's Press, 2006.

Leboutillier, Nate. *The Story of the Utah Jazz*. Mankato, MN: Creative Education, 2010.

Ray, Deborah Kogan. *Dinosaur Mountain: Digging into the Jurassic Age*. New York: Farrar, Straus, & Giroux, 2010.

WEBSITES

Utah Facts and Trivia:
http://www.50states.com/facts/utah.htm

Utah History for Kids:
http://www.ilovehistory.utah.gov/

Utah History to Go:
http://historytogo.utah.gov

Utah Kids:
http://www.utah.gov/education/kidspage.html

Utah Official State Website:
http://www.utah.gov

Utah State Capitol:
http://www.utahstatecapitol.utah.gov

Utah Travel Site:
http://www.utah.com

Doug Sanders lives in New York, where he writes and edits books for children. He has written several other titles in the It's My State! series, including Idaho, North Dakota, and Missouri.

Lisa M. Herrington, a former editor at *Weekly Reader*, has written numerous articles and books for children. She lives in Trumbull, Connecticut, with her husband and daughter.

INDEX

Page numbers in **boldface** are illustrations.